Endangered Animals Colouring Book

UK Amphibians and Reptiles

Activities for all ages

Supporting
Amphibian and Reptile Conservation Trust

Cassie Herschel-Shorland

My Fat Fox
MMXV

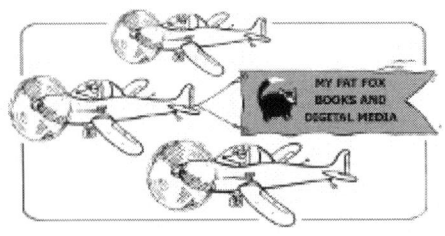

My Fat Fox
86 Gladys Dimson House
London E7 9DF
United Kingdom
www.myfatfox.co.uk

All rights reserved. No part of this publication may be used, reproduced, re–sold, lent, hired out, circulated or transmitted in any manner whatsoever, electronic or mechanical, in any form of binding or cover other than that in which it is published and without a similar condition including this condition being imposed on the subsequent purchaser without written permission from the author, except in the case of brief quotations embodied in articles or reviews.

Endangered Animals Colouring Book - UK Amphibians and Reptiles
Text and illustrations © 2015 Cassie Herschel-Shorland

The right of Cassie Herschel-Shorland to be identified as the author of this work has been asserted by her in accordance with the Copyright, Designs and Patents Act, 1988

Cover design
© 2015 Cassie Herschel-Shorland

ISBN 978-1-905747-46-7

*In fond memory of John Notton
and in appreciation of the beautiful colour and pattern
he showed me in the detail of nature*

Thank you to David Notton for support and advice

Contents

Introduction 1

About Amphibians and Reptiles 2

Endangered Amphibians of the United Kingdom 3

    Great Crested Newt *Triturus cristatus* 5

        A Year of Activity 9

    Natterjack Toad *Epidalea calamita* 13

    Pool Frog *Pelophylax lessonae* 17

Endangered Reptiles of the United Kingdom 21

    European Adder *Vipera berus* 23

    Grass Snake *Natrix natrix* 27

    Sand Lizard *Lacerta agilis* 31

    Slow Worm *Anguis fragilis* 35

Nature Notes 39

Snakes and Lizards: Colour and Play 43

Conservation Organizations 49

About the Illustrator 50

About My Fat Fox 51

Introduction

Colour is all around us and our natural world offers a spectacular range. Even animals we may describe as green, grey or brown offer an inspiring range of hues and tones in their detail. There's so much more to discover than just green in a Pool Frog and the brown Slow Worm is a surprise with the bright blues in its skin pattern.

There are seven native species of amphibians and six species of reptiles in the UK. All of the species in this colouring book are endangered or at risk. If any of these disappear due to extinction, we will also lose their amazing colours and a precious part of the natural world.

We would like to thank the Amphibian and Reptile Conservation Trust, especially Jim Foster their conservation director, for their support and advice and for their work to save these wonderful creatures.

A personal thank you also to Sam Bowring for excellent feedback on the game and to Karin Holloway for assistance with the text.

About Amphibians and Reptiles

Frogs, toads and newts are **amphibians**. They are cold-blooded animals which means they become the temperature that is around them. They have a backbone (a spinal column); they are vertebrates and so are we. Amphibians start life in water as eggs. They then grow to be larvae (tadpoles, with a tail), breathing through gills. The tadpole develops lungs and legs and then moves out of the water and onto land as an adult. Frogs, toads and newts have four toes (digits) on each front leg and five toes on each back leg. There are clues you can use to tell amphibians from reptiles: amphibians do not have scaly skin and they breed in water.

Lizards and snakes are **reptiles**. Like amphibians, reptiles are also cold-blooded vertebrates. Most reptiles lay soft-shelled eggs on land but some give birth to live young. Reptiles have five toes on each front leg and five toes on each back leg. A clue you can use to tell a reptile from an amphibian is the reptile's dry scaly skin.

Endangered Amphibians of the United Kingdom

Great Crested Newt
Triturus cristatus

The Great Crested Newt is sometimes called the Warty Newt. Its main feature is a tall crest along its back; the tail has crests on the top and underside. Adults can grow to about 12-14 cm (5 inches), including the tail!

Crested Newts are nocturnal and most active at night. In the day you might find one under stones or logs. They lay eggs in ditches, quarries and in ponds that don't have fish in them. Each egg is wrapped in a leaf or a blade of grass. Young newts prefer deep water ponds.

Their numbers fall as people pollute or destroy the Great Crested Newt's countryside breeding sites. More buildings and fewer ponds means fewer Great Crested Newts.

What can we do?
Great Crested Newts are protected by law and it is illegal to possess or handle them. Creating natural ponds and protecting their breeding grounds will help all newts to survive by having homes they are safe in.

What colour?
Crested newts are typically dark brown or grey-black and their colour is lighter during their breeding season. They have dark markings on their bodies and tails and they have white spots speckled on their head and sides. Their undersides are a striking orange or red with black or grey blotches.

A Year of Activity

The **amphibian life cycle**, from beginning to end, is a series of changes called metamorphosis. Very simply, they begin their life as an egg, covered in jelly, in a mass of eggs in shallow water. They change into tadpoles and swim in the water with tails and breathe under water with gills. They grow up and leave the water as small adults, hopping and walking on dry land with new legs and feet while breathing air through lungs. In the spring all adult amphibians in the UK return to still, fresh water to reproduce among water plants and create new spawn, as shown on the opposite page. They grow into full-size adults.

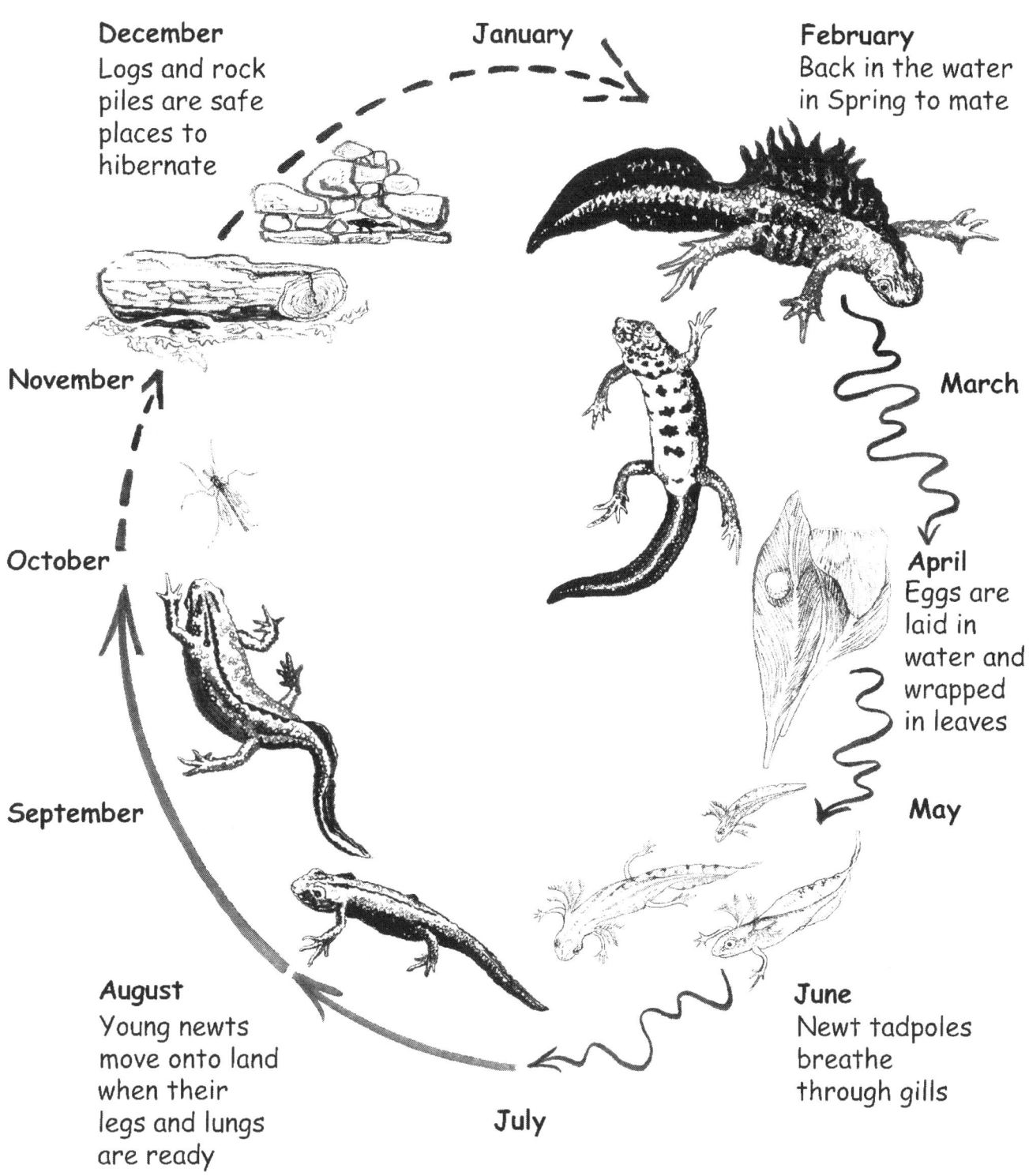

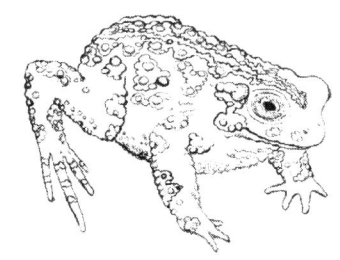

Natterjack Toad
Epidalea calamita

Natterjack Toads have short limbs and they run rather than hop. They can climb steep banks and dig burrows to hide in. After mating in ponds, they move to land and hunt in open spaces. The males can travel long distances to find new ponds using the Earth's magnetic field to navigate. Natterjack Toads are smaller than the Common Toad and can grow up to 10 cm (4 inches) long. Female Natterjack Toads are larger than the males.

Natterjack Toads are usually active at night when the males sing in chorus! They are happiest in sandy areas of heath, on coastal sand dunes or on river banks. If surprised, the toad's body inflates and its rump lifts up. They can also give off an unpleasant smell from their skin to ward off predators.

The toad's natural home is destroyed by housing development and by people illegally collecting them as pets.

What can we do?
Natterjack Toads are strictly protected by law; a licence is required to handle or disturb them. We can help them by maintaining, protecting and not disturbing the shallow ponds where they spawn.

What colour?
The Natterjack Toads' colours depend upon where they live. Usually, their upper surfaces are either pale brown or brownish-green. They have dark green, red, yellow or brown warts; their eyes are silvery-gold. Their most distinctive feature is a yellow stripe along the full length of its head and back. The underside of their body is creamy white with brown spots.

Pool Frog
Pelophylax lessonae

You might hear a Pool Frog before you see one! During the breeding season males make a loud call using a pair of inflatable pouches (vocal sacs), one on each side of their mouth. Adults are commonly 6.5 cm (2.5 inches) long but can grow up to 9 cm (3.5 inches).

The Pool Frog breeding season is May to June, much later in the year than the Common Frog. You might spot a Pool Frog basking in the sunshine on hot days in the summer but in winter they hide away on land to hibernate.

The Pool Frog is now recognised as a native British species. Their population has declined as air pollution causes over-nitrification of ponds and fewer people maintain ponds in towns or the countryside. People thought the Pool Frog was extinct in the wild in 1995! But there's good news for the 21st century – it is back again after being reintroduced in East Anglia.

What can we do?
The Pool Frog has full protection under European and UK native species law. It is an offence to kill, injure, or disturb them or to damage the Pool Frogs' habitats. It is also illegal to capture, sell or trade them at any stage of their life cycle.

People in East Anglia, where the pool frog has been reintroduced, can help by supporting wildlife groups and the Amphibian and Reptile Conservation Trust in their efforts to create more amphibian habitat.

What colour?
Pool Frogs' colours vary depending on where they live. In the UK, Pool Frogs have mostly greenish-brown backs with dark blotches. These blotches are dark brown on males and black on females. A yellow stripe runs down the centre of their back. Their sides are a yellow-green colour with darker spots. Their eyes are orange-yellow with large black pupils.

Endangered Reptiles of the United Kingdom

European Adder
Vipera berus

The **European Adder** is the only venomous UK reptile; they hatch complete with fangs and venom! Over time they learn how to use these for hunting. They inject the venom with their fangs to immobilize prey. Adders feed on smaller reptiles and mammals including voles, rats and mice. They are **very shy and pose little threat to humans unless they are threatened.** Adults typically grow to 40-70cm (16-28") in the UK. Adders give birth to live young.

They were once common in the UK but their hibernation sites, such as rabbit holes and under tree stumps, are being destroyed. Adders are a mysterious snake featured in literature from Arthurian legend to Shakespeare.

What can we do?
Adders are protected from being captured, killed or sold in the UK but they are not legally protected from disturbance. You can help Adders by increasing awareness that they are not a threat to humans and should not be harmed. Volunteer work with a local nature group is a fun way to help maintain natural habitat such as dry heathland and hedgerows.

What colour?
The distinctive features of an adder are its copper-coloured eyes, with vertical slit-shaped pupils, and the zigzag pattern along the full length of its back. Colour is variable but generally female Adders have a brown zigzag and males have a black zigzag. Their base colours can range from pale yellow to brown, orange or red.

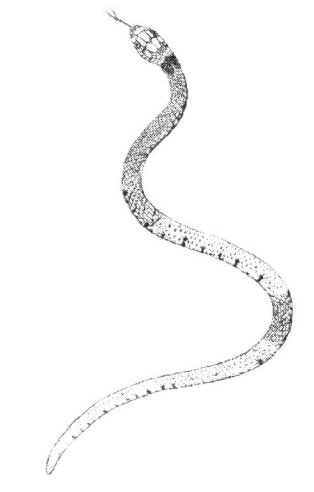

Grass Snake
Natrix natrix

The Grass Snake is Britain's largest reptile and may grow to over a metre (33") long. They swim and are often found in habitats featuring ponds, lakes, streams, marshes and ditches. They love to bask in the sunshine and can be spotted in open woodland, heathlands, gardens and parks.

Most live in the south and south east of England and Wales **and have recently been found in Scotland although their status here is uncertain.** There are no snakes in Ireland where legends say that snakes were expelled by Saint Patrick after they attacked him while fasting. However, there is no evidence in Irish fossil collections that snakes ever existed there.

Grass Snakes often play dead when threatened, possibly to dissuade predators from killing them. If caught the Grass Snake hisses loudly, releases a foul smell, and may strike with its head although it does not bite. They hunt for frogs, toads and newts, swallowing them whole.

What can we do?
The Grass Snake is fully protected by law against being sold, injured or killed in the UK. The conservation strategy for this species is to educate people about the snake and to encourage people to accept its presence.

What colour?
Grass Snakes are typically olive-green, brown or greyish in colour. A variable row of black marks run underside and along its sides; each Grass Snake has unique markings. Occasionally it has smaller dark round markings along the back in double rows. The species is sometimes called the Ringed Snake because of a distinctive black and yellow collar behind the head. The underside is off-white or yellowish with dark triangular or rectangular markings

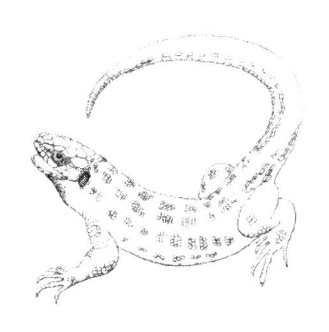

Sand Lizard
Lacerta agilis

There are only three types of native lizard in the UK and the **Sand Lizard** is the rarest. They have powerful short legs, distinctive blunt heads and an aggressive bite. Sand Lizards also have a distinctive forked tongue. They can grow to about 15-24 cm (6-10 inches) length and their tail is about one-and-a-half times longer than their body!

Sand Lizards are shy of humans but sociable with other Sand Lizards. They often share tunnels that they have taken over from mice or voles.

In the wild they are only found in protected heathland sites and on protected sand dune systems. But they can also be found along railway lines, roadways, field boundaries and on brownfield sites. Sand Lizards bask in the sun on sand or on vegetation close to the ground, warming-up to hunt. They dig burrows to bury their eggs, where they are then safe and warm. This is also where Sand Lizards hibernate over winter.

Large birds, badgers, cats and foxes hunt the Sand Lizard. Its habitat is destroyed by wild fires and building on heathland, modern farming, and sand or gravel extraction. Found only on a few sites, the Sand Lizard is therefore declining in the UK.

What can we do?
Sand Lizards are protected by law. It is illegal to kill, possess or sell them. You can support Sand Lizards by joining a local wildlife trust or volunteer group.

What colour?
Sand Lizard colours vary and are either a pale grey or a sandy-brown colour. You might recognise a male Sand Lizard by its brilliant green sides when it changes colour during the mating season. They all have a repeated pattern of irregular dark brown blotches along their back and sides which are highlighted with a single white fleck in the centre of the blotch. The white flakes join-up to form striped patterns.

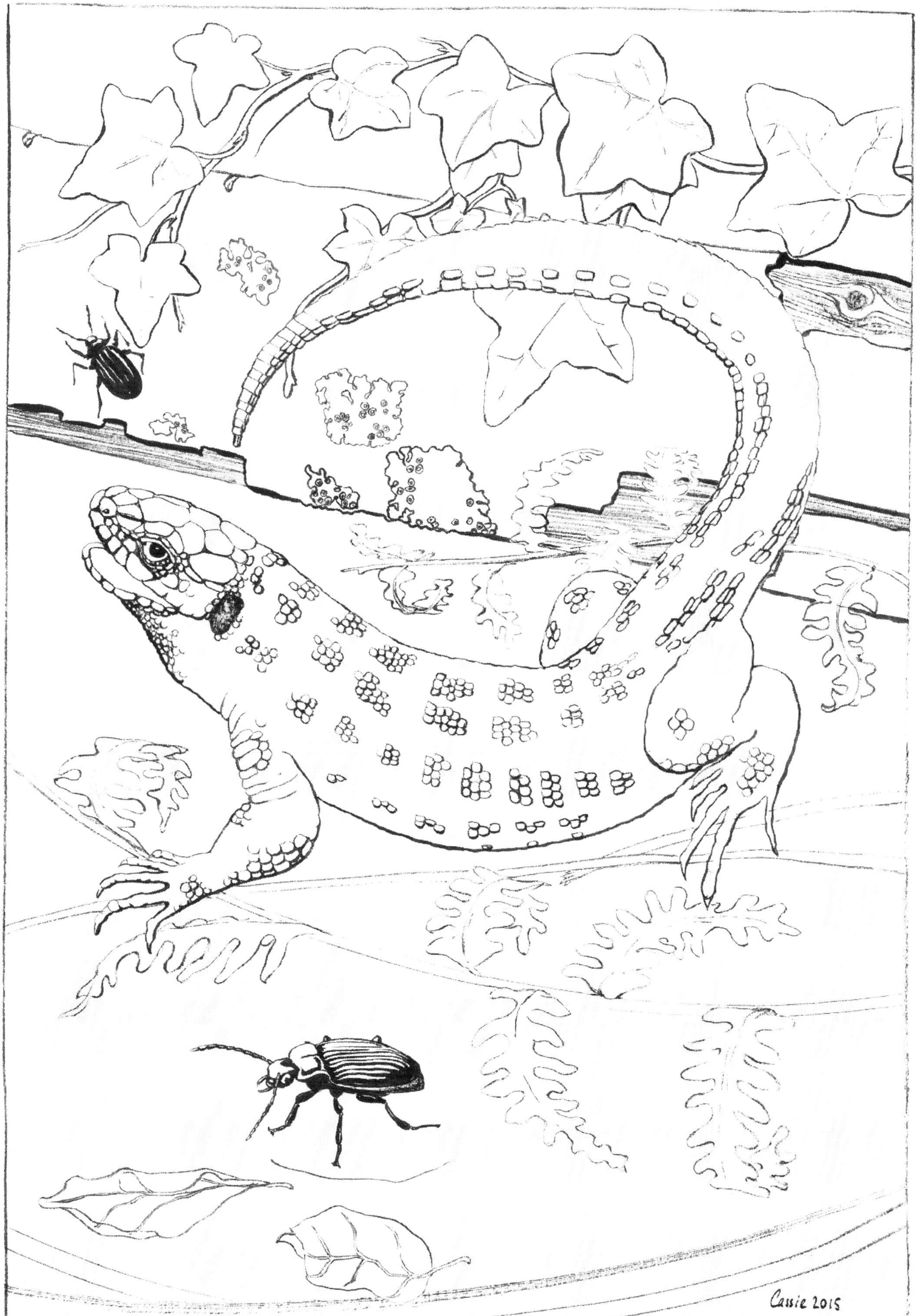
Cassie 2015

Slow Worm
Anguis fragilis

The **Slow Worm** is a legless lizard! They can shed their tails to escape from predators and, unlike snakes, they can blink with their eyelids. They have visible ears and a rounded, notched tongue. Adults can grow to about 50 cm (20 inches) long. Some of them live up to 30 years in the wild. Slow Worms give birth to live young.

You might find one in your garden if it is damp and untidy! They often hunt snails and slugs in compost heaps. Slow Worms are widespread across the UK but rare in places with cats, which may hunt and kill them.

What can we do?
Slow Worms are protected by law in the UK and are classified as a Priority Species in the UK Biodiversity Action Plan. Don't keep an outdoor cat!

What colour?
Slow Worms are glassy smooth and shiny. Males and females look different. Males may be greyish, brown, coppery or reddish brown and they don't have any stripes. Some of them have blue spots. Female Slow Worms may be brown, copper-coloured, or red on the back with brown or black sides that have light iridescent flecks. Many females have a dark stripe down the middle of their back and stripes running along the sides of their body. Very rare Slow Worms are entirely black and extremely rare ones have no pigment (albino).

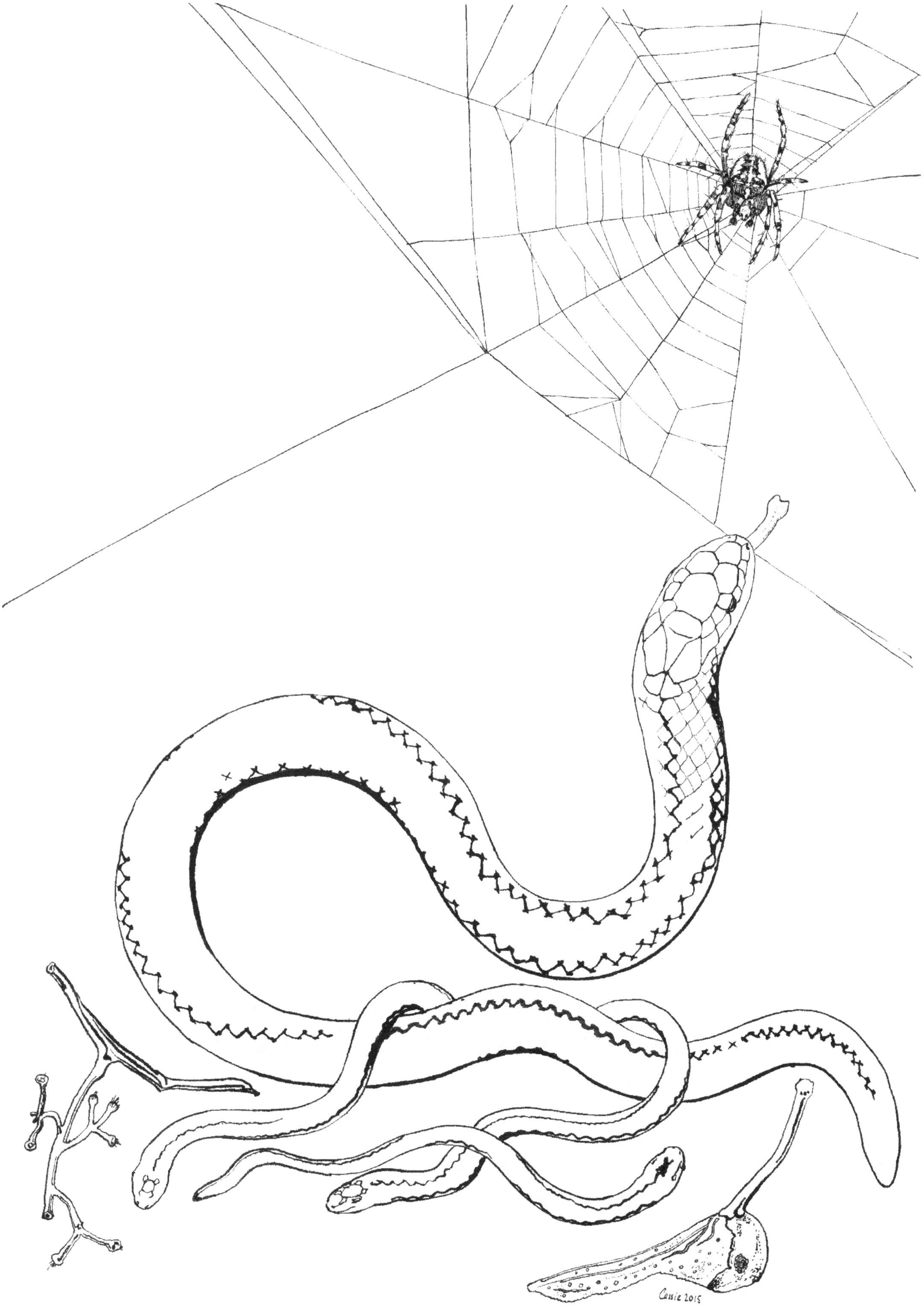
Cassie 2015

Nature Notes

The loss of UK heathland and grassland habitats through human activity threatens the survival of reptiles. The Wildlife Trusts are working closely with planners, developers and farmers to ensure natural habitats are protected by fostering Living Landscape schemes.

You can create a log pile in your garden for amphibians to hibernate beneath. In partnership with the RHS, The Wildlife Trust's 'Wild About Gardens' initiative can help you plan your own wildlife garden.

You can also help protect, encourage and monitor UK amphibians and reptiles by joining a local wildlife group in your area or by **volunteering for and/or supporting the Amphibian and Reptile Conservation Trust.** Your observations can be added to the national network of sightings. To take field notes during your observations take a note-pad, pencil and a magnifier with you and be careful not to disturb your subject!

Nature notes

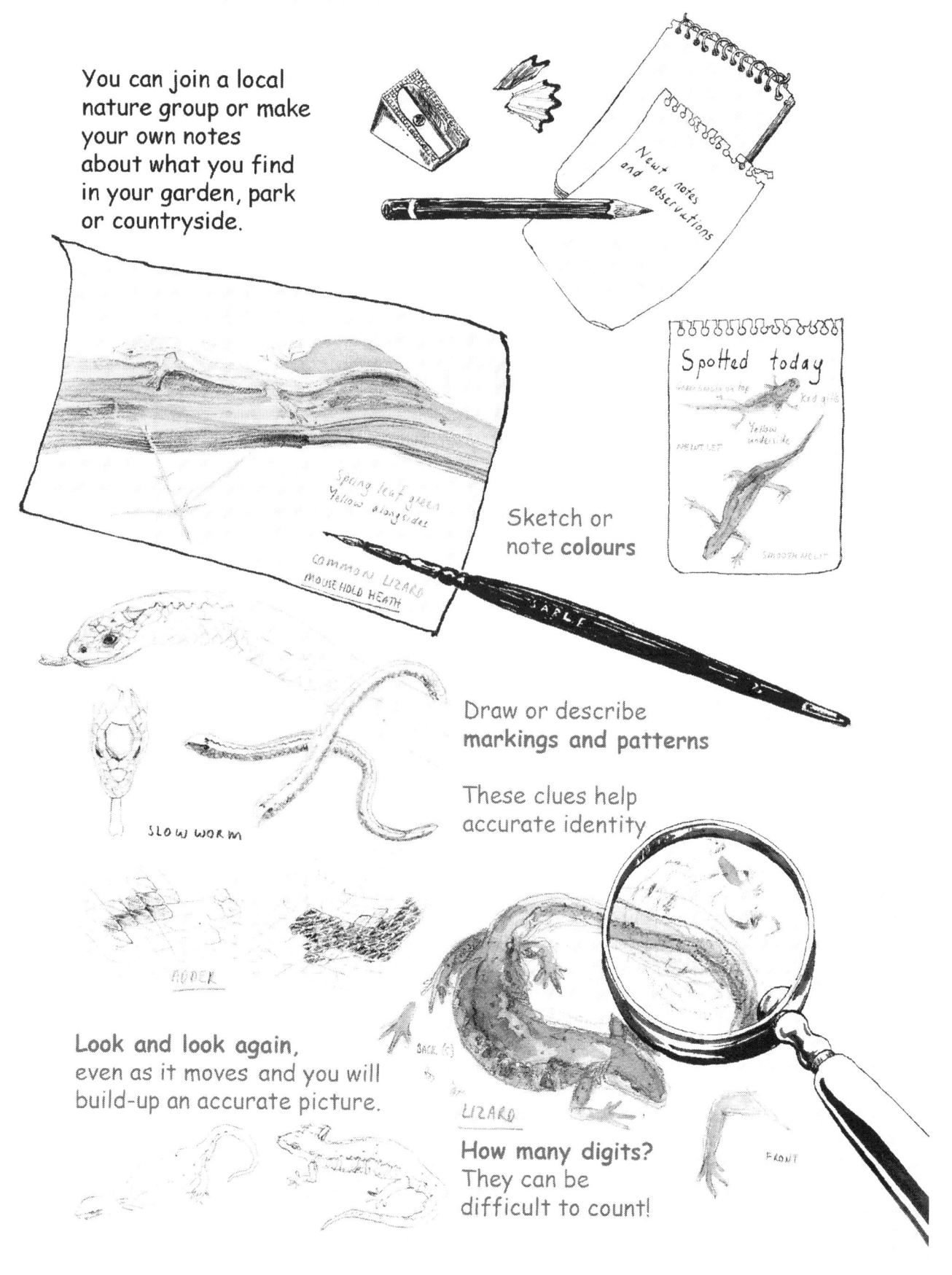

You can join a local nature group or make your own notes about what you find in your garden, park or countryside.

Newt notes and observations

Spotted today

Sketch or note **colours**

Draw or describe **markings and patterns**

These clues help accurate identity

Look and look again, even as it moves and you will build-up an accurate picture.

How many digits? They can be difficult to count!

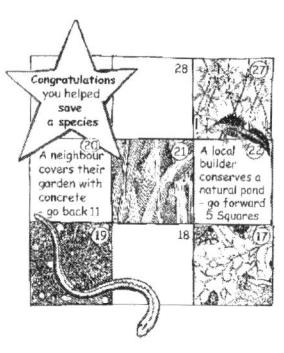

Snakes and Lizards: Colour and Play

Snakes and Lizards is a board game to colour and play. It's based on the 'Snakes and Ladders' game. It could inspire ideas on how you, your friends and family might help to save a species.

Snakes and Lizards

Adder

Great Crested Newt

Natterjack Toad

Sand Lizard

Pool Frog

Get ready to play

Colour and **cut out** these **counters**

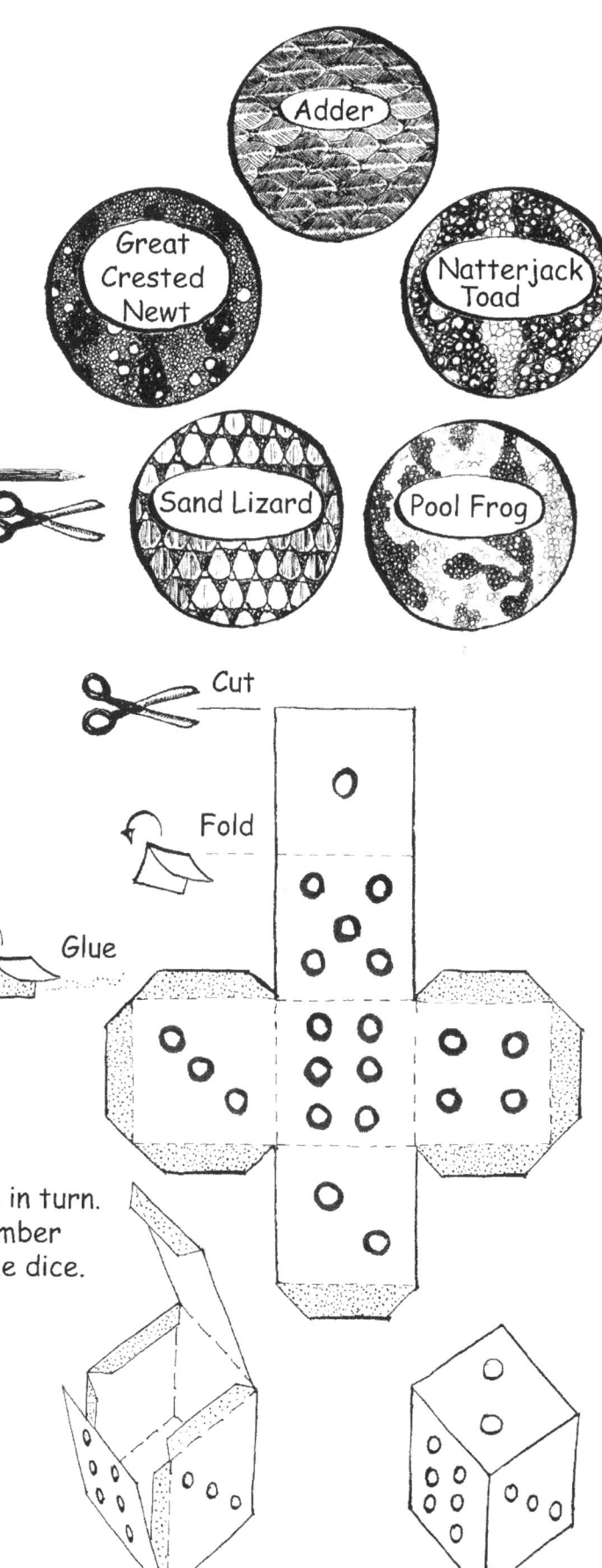

You can use your own **dice** or
colour, cut, fold and glue this template to make one.

Cut

Fold

Glue

How to play

Select a 'counter'.

Throw the dice in turn. The first person to throw a 6 starts.

Each player throw the dice in turn. Move forward the same number of squares as number on the dice.

If you land on an action then move forward or go back as instructed.

You can colour the game, too!

Snakes and Lizards

Congratulations you helped save a species

25 Sand lizard sold in local pet shop – go back 2 squares

20 A neighbour covers their garden with concrete – go back 11

22 A local builder conserves a natural pond – go forward 5 Squares

23 for Sale

16 Camp fire destroys a nature area – go back 9 squares

14 Lizards in your wildlife patch – go forward 1 square

4 Toads migrate through your garden – go forward 4 squares

Start here to help save a species

Conservation Organizations

If you would like to help UK amphibians and reptiles, please consider joining and/or donating money to these organisations:

ARC Amphibian and Reptile Conservation Trust: **www.arc-trust.org/**

Act for Wildlife – Amphibian Conservation Project, Chester Zoo: **www.actforwildlife.org.uk/amphibians/**

ARGUK – Amphibian and Reptile Groups of the UK: **www.arguk.org/**

BIAZA – British and Irish Association of Zoos and Aquariums: **www.biaza.org.uk/**

Born Free – Keep Wildlife in the Wild: **www.bornfree.org.uk/**

British Herpetological Society: **www.thebhs.org/**

British Wildlife Rehabilitation Council: **bwrc.org.uk/**

Dudley Zoological Gardens: **www.dudleyzoo.org.uk/**

Durrell Wildlife Conservation Trust: **www.durrell.org/**

Froglife: **www.froglife.org/**

Herpetological Society of Ireland: **thehsi.org/**

The Wildlife Trusts: **www.wildlifetrusts.org/**

Whitley Wildlife Conservation Trust: **www.wwct.org.uk/**

About the Illustrator

Cassie Herschel-Shorland's artistic works present visual interpretations of our heritage.

Her illustrations are based on observation and research. Whether her subject is natural history or science, the intention is joy in the discovery of detail and personal connections as well as in learning about the wider wonders of our world.

Cassie has an MA in Archaeological Illustration and Historical Reconstruction. Cassie has developed her skills in capturing and sharing often overlooked aspects of the past and present in visual formats while working in museums and galleries. Creating activity books is another expression of Cassie's ability to delight and engage both children and adults in natural and cultural heritage.

My Fat Fox has also published Cassie's beautiful book, 'Where Do the Swallows Go?', a delightfully illustrated book that follows swallows on their long journey from South Africa to Europe and back. Available from Amazon and other booksellers.

About My Fat Fox

My Fat Fox is a small independent publisher of books and digital media. We are in love with our world and hope to encourage others to fall in love with it too.

More from My Fat Fox

Endangered Lizards Colouring Book
Endangered Frogs Colouring Book
Illustrated by Jay Manchand

Colour to Save the Ocean – Book One
Colour to Save the Ocean – Book Two
Illustrated by Kasia Niemczynska

Color and Save the Ocean – Book One
Saving Animals in Costa Rica – Sibu Sanctuary
Party Animals Coloring Book – Mollywood
Illustrated by Karin Hoppe Holloway

Color Funny Doodles – Book One – Humorous
Color Funny Doodles – Book Two – Beautiful
Illustrated by Hartmut Jager

Colour Me Alan! Ten Small Steps to Be a Hog Hero!!!
Illustrated by Jon Hitchman

Where Do the Swallows Go?
Illustrated by Cassie Herschel-Shorland

A portion of the proceeds from all our Earth Art Apps colouring books are donated to conservation organizations. Each book has more details of which organization it supports and what proportion of the proceeds will be donated.

Visit **www.myfatfox.co.uk** for competitions, news and information on our latest publications.

All our colouring books will soon be available as Earth Art Apps.

Printed in Great Britain
by Amazon